THE BIG BOOK OF

Favourite
Yorkshire Tales

First published in Great Britain in 2012 by Dalesman Publishing
an imprint of
Country Publications Ltd
The Water Mill, Broughton Hall
Skipton, North Yorkshire BD23 3AG

ISBN 978-1-85568-306-8

Printed in China by Latitude Press Ltd.

Introduction

Over the years many magazines have come and gone, but few have lasted as long and so well as *Dalesman*. When the magazine was first published in 1939 it did not appear to have been a very wise decision. War was looming, and upon the onset of hostilities there was an acute shortage of paper. Despite this, not a single issue missed being published. Perhaps it was the enthusastic welcome penned by the Bradford-born author J B Priestley which ensured success for the first issue.

The main reason, however, why *Dalesman* has been so successful is because of its contributors. It has always been the mix of humour and nostalgia which has been its appeal.

During the compiling of this book, I have been privileged to read through all the back issues of *Dalesman*, as well as its sister magazine *Down Your Way*. Whilst working on the book I was reminded of the minister whose congregation had complained at the length of the sermon. His reply? "If that knew what I'd left aht, that wouldn't complain at what Ah'd put in."

I felt the same, and the tales and poems in this volume had to be selected from many thousands of words, complemented by a small selection from many hundreds of equally comical cartoons.

What shines through these pages at all times is the humour typical of our wonderful county – Yorkshire.

RON FREETHY

Makkin' a Hen-Hoil
Will Clemence

Ah've swapped all me rabbits for pullets
An' gotten a duck in me swap
Theel make brass wi eggs – soah the tell me;
Well Ah'm aht for owt Ah can cop.

But fowls tak mo-er room up ner rabbits
An' ducks like to spread aht an' all:
So Ah've built a gurt hen hoil in't gardin
Wi a duckery ligged ageean't wall.

Ah ran a bit short makkin' t' hen hoil
Ah'd cadged biggest part o' me wood:
An' me saw war as blunt as me manners
So t' job wadn't finished so good.

Ah used nearly all t' wood on t' hen-hoil;
Its roof reyches up to me chin:
So at t' size o' yon duck-hoil hes suffered:
Nah t' duck has to duck to gerrin.

Visitor: "What's that new building on the fell?"
Farmer: "If I can find a tenant, it's a bungalow; if not, it's a barn."

IN THE early days, a mill owner from Batley became very rich. He was determined to have the best house in Yorkshire. He could hardly read or write but he could afford to pay the best architect.

The architect asked him which aspect he would like.

The mill owner asked: " 'As 'im up road gitten an aspect?" referring to one of his rivals.

The architect pointed out that each house had to have an aspect.

"Reet then," came the reply. "Tha'd better gi' me three."

IT WAS in Swaledale that a farmer put through a phone call.

"Ah want yan-nuthin'-nought-nowt please miss."

It speaks well for the local exchange that it got the number one thousand.

A lazy farmer was said to be able "to fill a bed and empty a cupboard" and "'e's over tiered to goa to sleep."

THERE WAS a lad in a Dales village who was not particularly bright, but he was a friendly chap. One day some of the other lads decided to take him to see a football match as he had never seen one, and could not understand the game when they explained it.

He was wide-eyed with amazement at the sight, first of the spectators in their thousands, and then of twenty-two men in short pants trotting on to the field.

As the teams lined up for the kick-off he wanted to know what that chap did under that bar between those two props. And he just couldn't believe that all he did was to stop the ball from passing between the posts.

"Heaw mich dus that chap get fur this job?"

"Abaut £20."

"Heck. Ah know a joiner up eaur street as'll board up that oppenin' fur less ner half that money."

IF YOU can't get to sleep start counting sheep, try to do it the Wharfedale way.

1 = yan
2 = tan
3 = tether
4 = pathas
5 = pimp
6 = setha
7 = letha
8 = hova
9 = dova
10 = dik
11 = yan-a-dick
12 = tan-a-dick
13 = tethra-dick
14 = petha-dick
15 = bomfit
16 = yan-a-bomfit
17 = tan-a-bomfit
18 = teth-a-bomfit
19 = patj-a-bomfit
20 = gigit

It may be Scandinavian in origin. Some think this goes back even further to the Celtic language.

The Sheffield artist, delivering his latest commission to a client – a portrait of the client's wife – was asked why he had used a particular painting technique. He replied: "I painted her in oils 'cos she looks like a sardine".

A FARMER, after going round to feed his cattle, and milk his cows, in winter time when it was dark, instead of opening the door would knock and wait for his wife to open it. His wife, of course, would answer the door, thinking that it was a neighbour who had come to see them. This happened several times, after which his wife got a bit annoyed. So one night there was the usual knock at the door and, being upstairs, called out from the top of the stairs:

"Coom in, thee ould silly devil."

Imagine her surprise when the door opened and in came the vicar.

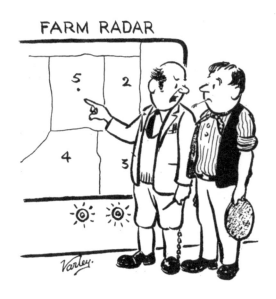

"What's that weed doing in t' middle of t' five-acre pasture?"

Washday, Mussels for Tea
Susan Thompson

Old black range burning bright,
Heats the water through the night.
Possing and turning, sheets a-tangle,
Out from the tub, and through the mangle.

Washday treat, mussels for tea,
Cooked on the hob, for you and me.
Water ladled from the tub,
Mangle moved and well scrubbed.

Clothes hung out on the line,
Hard work finished for a time.
Rest and ease for the night,
Until again the fire to light.

LETTING IN the New Year or 'first footing' is still the custom in Yorkshire and invariably the job is given to a dark-haired man, and preferably a bachelor.

In years gone by there was an agreeable custom of giving gloves as a New Year's present but this custom has long since vanished. There was also a custom of making New Year resolutions but the habit of keeping them has also long since vanished.

It was firmly believed that if your pockets are empty over the New Year then poverty would be your companion over the whole year ahead. One Tyke remembers his great grandmother having a half-farthing in every pocket which was passed on from one generation to the next. This coin went out of circulation in 1844.

Another superstition is that nothing must be moved from a house on New Year's Day, and it was considered very bad luck if your fire is allowed to go out during New Year's Eve and many a chap ran home during the pre-midnight festivities to 'stoke up'. There was even a superstition regarding drinks taken at New Year. Whoever drinks the last dregs from a bottle will have good luck for the rest of the year.

THE FARMER sent a very young and inexperienced Land Girl muck-carting.

"He's a quiet horse," the farmer said, "but he doesn't like the rein to touch his back."

"We had one or two showers," the Land Girl said when she returned, "but I held my mac over him."

A DALES farmer had to undergo a rather serious operation. This was performed by an eminent Leeds surgeon and was successful. The time came for the farmer to pay the surgeon's fee.

"How much dost ta want?" asked the farmer.

"Fifty guineas," said the surgeon.

The farmer proceeded to count out the notes laboriously.

"Oh please," said the surgeon. "Give me a cheque and save yourself a lot of trouble."

"Nay, nay," said the farmer. "Ah've put thee down in my income tax as ten loads o' muck."

DALES TWANG: When is a sheep not a sheep?

Lamb: Term for a sheep until it has been separated from its mother.

Hogg: Stage after a lamb, until first shearing.

Gimmer: Term for a female sheep.

Wether: A male, castrated for use as a fattening animal.

Shearling: A sheep after the first clipping.

Tup: A male sheep kept for breeding.

GRANDPA WAS dying, and his wife, having to leave him alone while she went to the shop, turned out the light. "We mun save us brass, lad," she told him.

"Then leave me a candle," he pleaded.

"Well – all reight then – but if tha feels thisenn goin', blow it aht.

A FARMER with a small milk round had killed an old hen for a customer, but had no scales on which to weigh it. He sent his young daughter with the hen to the next farm with the request that the farmer's wife should weigh it on her butter scales. The child returned with the hen and this tale:

"Mary Ann says t' hen weighs a four pound weight, a yetter [an instrument used for heating old type starching irons], a big onion and a pot egg."

A SCOTSMAN married a Yorkshire woman and they set up house in the Dales. Two sons were born. "They're half Yorkshire and half Scots," he told a friend. "They're thrifty lads. They can save. That's Scots. But it's my money they save. That's Yorkshire."

A DALESMAN won first prize in a lottery – a pony and trap. The organisers of the lottery brought the prize and the lucky winner came out into the street to inspect it. After a bit he said: "Ay, ah knew ther'd be a catch in it someweere. There's no whip."

THE BEST man was doing his utmost to keep spirits high at a wedding when he noticed a gloomy looking chap in the corner. "Not enjoying yourself?" he asked. "Have you kissed the lovely bride yet?"

The man gave him a faraway look and said "Not lately."

"Can you spare a few coppers?"

A LOCAL preacher who conducted a service at a small Dales chapel where the congregation numbered two – a senile man and the chapel-keeper-cum-organist – was told by the latter, as she made her way to the organ:

"Cut the sermon short when tha' smells t' Yorksher pudding."

A DALES farmer, well known for his excessive thrift, was on his way to Skipton market when he called at the local blacksmith to have a foreign body removed from his eye. The blacksmith stopped work and with a sharpened match performed the operation. Then, holding up the fly impaled on the match, asked:

"Will ter teck it wi' thee or call fer it as tha comes back?"

Hirin' Day
W G Walmsley

It's a gurt strappin' lad I's am wantin'
A lad 'at can do a day's wark
One 'at can milk when 'e's axed to:
And yoke up a hoss in a cart.
Does ta knaw that a farmer's lad nivver ligs in:
That tha' moan't fell a tree when in sap
That tha' woan't use a hammer, no more than
  tha's forced
When tha once sets a gate in a gap
Does ta know that gilt, gimmer and cob are
  all names
'At a farmer mun gives to 'is stock?
An' tha knows that a pullet is just a young hen
An' a cockerel is just a young cock.
If tha'll do reet wi me tha'll find a good shop
Tak hod o' this bob and tha's hired
But start laikin' on, and at end o' thi term
Tha'll danged sooin find out that tha's fired.

A GROUP of forty-year-old girlfriends discussed where they should meet for dinner and agreed on Ocean View restaurant because the waiters there had tight pants and nice bottoms.

Ten years later at fifty, the group once again discussed where to meet for dinner, finally choosing the same restaurant because the food and wine were excellent.

As sixty-year-olds they met up again, and again picked Ocean View for dinner because of the peace and quiet and beautiful view.

Ten years on at seventy, they again discussed where to dine and again agreed on the very same restaurant because it had wheelchair access and a lift.

At the grand old age of eighty, the group again asked themselves where to go for that special meal – and agreed they must go to the Ocean View restaurant because they had never been there before.

A DALESWOMAN walked into a grocer's shop and the following conversation took place.

Woman: "Do you sell paraffin?"

Assistant: "Yes ma'am."

Woman: "Do you sell firelighters?"

Assistant: "Yes ma'am."

Woman: "Well thee go aht an' wash thi 'ands. Then I'll hev twa ounce of boiled ham."

QUEUING TO pay for her supermarket groceries, the little old lady was asked if she had brought her own shopping bag as giving out masses of plastic bags wasn't very environmentally-friendly. She apologised and added: "No, we didn't have this green thing in my day."

The cashier replied censoriously: "That's the problem... previous generations just didn't do enough to save our planet."

"But, wait a minute," the old lady reminded her accuser, "back then we returned our milk, pop and beer bottles to the shop which sent them to be washed, sterilised and refilled – and we used them over and over again.

"We washed the baby's nappies because we didn't have the throwaway kind and we dried clothes outside, not in an energy burning machine or on a central heating radiator. And we washed all our stuff by hand, and in the kitchen we stirred and mixed by hand, and we cut the lawn by a push mower.

"We didn't have disposable this and that; Dad got a new blade for his razor when the old one became dull. We refilled our pens with ink instead of buying a new one. If something got broken, it was repaired by Dad, or by brother, or by a kindly neighbour – and not immediately ditched in the dustbin.

"We recycled our clothes too; they were handed down the family – we rarely got new ones.

"And we walked everywhere and didn't climb into a car to go a couple of miles down the road to school or shops. In any case, few mums and dads even possessed a car. Or we took the bus or a bike.

"And there wasn't a radio, TV or computer blazing away in every room...and when we got a TV it had a screen the size of a handkerchief, not the size of a house wall."

By now the lengthening queue had broken into spontaneous applause. Maybe the oldies did know a thing or two about saving the planet after all.

THERE IS a story of Murgatroyd Dickinson, known as Mog Dick, who lived in Oakworth in the 1800s. He was fearful of being robbed and he kept his coins in a frying pan covered in fat. When he went out shopping he melted the fat and took out what he needed. Is this an old version of liquid assets?

ON 4TH AUGUST 1928 a huge meat and potato pie was paraded through the village of Denby Dale and it took hundreds of people to eat it. On 21st September 1940 the metal dish was sold for scrap to help in the war effort. It attracted more than fifty bidders and raised £72.17 shillings.

A LITTLE boy was sent to spend a few days with his aunt. Hoping to make the child feel at home, she put him in a chair, placed her cat on his lap and showed the child how to stroke the cat. Not long afterwards the lady was reassured that all was well when the little lad called out delightedly: "Eeh, Auntie Ellen, this cat's buzzin'."

LITTLE GIRL: "I think when I go to Heaven I'd like to take a cow."

Mother: "But cows are not allowed in Heaven."

Little girl: "Then who has to go down to Hell for the milk?"

THE VILLAGE butcher gazed sadly at the farmer's wife who complained about the bone in the meat. Then he offered her this consolation:

"Tha' knaws if tha' buys meat tha' buys bone; if tha' buys eggs tha' buys shells; if tha' buys fruit tha' buys stone; an if tha' buys beer tha' buys nowt else."

A MAN who wrote and asked whether a hotel in Settle permitted dogs had the following reply:

"I've been in the hotel business for over thirty years. Never yet have I had to call the police to eject a disorderly dog in the wee small hours of the morning. No dog has ever passed a dud cheque on me. Never yet has a dog set the bedclothes alight from smoking in bed. No dog has ever failed to pay his bar bill. I've never found a hotel blanket or cutlery in a dog's suitcase. Your dog's welcome.

"PS. If the dog will vouch for you, then you can come as well."

POLICE STOPPED an old man tottering around the streets in the early hours and asked him where he was going?

"I'm going to a lecture on alcohol abuse," he replied.

"Oh really, and where would that be this time of night?" asked the officer.

"It'll be by the missus when I get home," he said.

LEGEND HAS it that Titus Salt stood on top of the knoll, a small hill north of Shipley, and gazed along the Aire Valley. His eyes rested on a point where railway and canal ran close together amid beautiful surroundings, and said to himself:

"This is where I am going to build the most wonderful mill in Europe."

The mill was built – he called it "a palace of industry" – and with it a complete village providing revolutionary accommodation and amenities for the workers. The village was called Saltaire and is a memorial to a man of vision and foresight.

Titus Salt – the very name has a ring of greatness to it – was in fact one of the most interesting personalities of the whole Victorian era. Born in 1803 he began work at the age of seven as a Bradford wool stapler in the early days of steam-driven mills. It was not until he was thirty-three that Titus made a discovery which was to put him way ahead of his contemporaries.

It happened in a Liverpool warehouse where some 300 dirty-looking bales of alpaca, a wool that comes from the mountain tops of Peru and Chile, were lying on the floor and were about to be shipped back to South America as unsaleable.

Titus smuggled some of the material away in a handkerchief and locked himself into a room. He scoured and combed the alpaca, and saw the grubby fibres transformed into a long and glossy wool, which proved to be ideal for the light fancy fabrics then in great demand. He promptly bought all the 300 bales at the rate of 8d a pound. Within three years the quantity imported rose to £2,000,000 a year and the price to 2s 6d a pound.

Charles Dickens, no stranger to Yorkshire, embroidered the warehouse incident into *Household Words*, and invented the beautiful Dickensian name of CW & F Foozle and Company for a firm of Liverpool brokers. He wrote:

"He [Titus] looked at it [the alpaca] felt it, rubbed it, pulled it about. In fact he did all but taste it – he would have done this if it had suited his purpose, for he was Yorkshire."

A SMALL boy, who had been promised a baby brother or sister for his birthday:

"If it doesn't make you too big, Mummy, I'd like a Shetland pony too."

TWO DRUNKS were walking home along the railway line between Huddersfield and Dewsbury.

"There's a heck of a lot of steps," remarked the first drunk.

His equally inebriated pal replied: "I'll tell thi what's worse, this handrail is too low".

"There are only five jobs in looking after pigs: three of them are disgusting, and two are dull."

TWO DALES farming families were constantly having arguments. The two families passed each other with difficulty along a narrow road. Both had cars piled high.

One shouted: "Ah see thou's flittin'."

"Aye," came the reply.

The first farmer's wife spoke up from within the car: "Well if they're flittin' we might as well go home agin."

A YOUNG couple in the early 1880s were courting. They had a tiff but eventually got together again. An older fisherwoman said that all would be well. It would be like 'saut fish' (salted fish) – it was better when warmed up.

The Dalesman's Games

Ah'd like ter see some country sports
Wi' t' farm stock takkin' part;
A huss rail just for hosses:
Noh jockeys – they'd do baht.
A tug-o' wurm between two ducks
A hurdle race for hares
A boxin' match for rabbits
Wi'em soarta aht i' pairs.
A tuppin' match for billy goats
An' wrassling fer cows;
An' just to mek things even:
A special thing for t' sows.
They'd have a contest o' the'r awn;
An' this 'ud be me plan.
First prize 'ud goe to onny pig
'As cowt a greasy man.

A BOW-LEGGED stranger came into a Dales pub, obviously wet and cold. When he occupied the best place by the fire, nobody objected until he had been there for more than an hour. Then an old lad whose place it usually was tapped him on the shoulder and pointed to his legs.

"Sithee lad," he said. "Move thissen back a bit. Tha's warpin."

THE LOCAL publican was umpiring a cricket match. Early in his innings the batsman was hit on his pads yards outside the leg stump. An excited fielder shouted: "How's that?"

Up went the publican's hand and to the astonishment of spectators he yelled:

"Out you dammed tee-totaller."

THE COALMAN in the Dales was met in the street by one of his customers who joyfully shouted:

"Ah say Joe. Ah shan't want them coals I ordered from thee t' other day."

"How's that?"

"Ah'm flittin'."

"Yes," said Joe, "but you'll want coals theer just t' same."

"Noa. T' house we're goin' to hes gotten hot and cold watter."

"Psst! Try blowing up its nostrils."

OLD GEORGE was ill and feeling sorry for himself. His wife Martha was going shopping. Says he:

"Martha Ah's ga'an ta dee. Fetch me an ounce of baccy."

"Nay," says she. "If these ga'an ta dee, hawf an ounce 'll be plenty."

WHILST WATCHING over the collection in a Yorkshire chapel the steward was surprised when a youth put a shilling into the box and calmly counted out eleven pence change.

NONT SARAH'S is one of those landmark pubs, gloriously sited at 1,155 feet above sea level overlooking bleak moor, Scammonden Dam and its sailing club, and, of course, the M62. What of its name?

The story goes that many years ago a Scammonden native, who had the chance of a pub in Lancashire but was short of cash, sought and got a loan from an aunt. He did well, bought the moorland pub and out of gratitude named it Nont Sarah's.

Maple panelling from the *Mauretania*, once the biggest and fastest ocean liner, can be found in the pub. Once a smartly dressed American on a cotton delegation came into the tap room, looked as if he'd entered paradise, and said:

"Boys, have a drink on me. I've just seen a bit of England such as I wanted to see."

What had he seen? Sixty-five hams hanging from the beams.

Rumour has it that Nont Sarah returns occasionally to check her investment.

OLD SUSANNAH, when she was out of sorts: "Ah's off me eggs an' onto cawd tetties."

A MINER'S widow of ample proportions had died during a heatwave in August. Her daughter, on being offered condolences, replied that they feared her mother "wouldn't keep for t' funeral, so we had to salt her a bit."

AN OLD woman in Carlton had a husband who was ill and very near his end.

A friend said:

"You must be tired with all this nursing and extra work."

"Aye," she replied. "I mun get off to Morecambe when I get 'im putten aways."

A DALESMAN died and, making arrangements for his funeral, his widow, Matilda, called at the local barbers.

Matilda: "Will ta come an' shave our John for t' buryin?"

Barber: "All reet – it'll be hawf a crahn."

Matilda: "Ah thowt tha nobbut charged thrippence."

Barber: "Ay thrippence for wick'uns, but it's half a crahn for corpses."

Matilda: "Can't tha dew it for less? Ah mun be careful nah. Ah've nowt but t' insurance an' mi' pension."

Barber: "Sorry Matilda, but Ah'm nooan doin' deead uns for less."

Matilda: "Then Ah weean't bother. He's nooan going onywheer."

OVERHEARD ON a Whitby bus:

"Aye, Dr Brash 'ee sed ter me: 'Yer don't want to eat ser many fried sausages the're nah good for thee blood pressure,' and dusta kna it's tekin' some gitten' used to eaten 'em raw."

A BRADFORD mill owner was waiting for a train on a platform at Crossflats. He also had a farm and he 'made brass' by taking his surplus eggs to sell to his millworkers. He dropped an egg but picked it up and put it in the lid of his thermos flask. One of his fellow travellers gasped at this and said:

"Tha's nut goin' to eat it?"

"Nivver thee mind," he replied. "It'll poach."

He died a millionaire.

A daleswoman was angry with her daughter. "So tha's broke a saucer, has ter? Ah don't kna what thi father will say when 'e 'as to drink out of 'is cup."

A DALESMAN got into an empty train carriage, and at the next stop a battle-axe of a woman got in and glared at the old chap preparing to light his pipe.

"May I tell you," she said, "that smoking makes me ill."

The dalesman waited until his pipe was well alight before he replied.

"Does it lass. Then tha shud tak my advice an' give it up."

"I could repair it in a jiffy, sir, but I'm afraid the computer says three-and-a-half days."

A MAN was travelling along a Dales road in thick fog. A dalesman loomed up and the driver asked: "Which is the best way to Thirsk?" The local told him. Twenty miles and two hours later the driver saw another dalesman.

"Which way to Thirsk?" he asked.

"Nay lad," he replied. "Ah've telt thee yance."

A GARAGE owner in the North Riding tells of an old lady who complained that her new car was using too much fuel. He pointed to the choke lever which was fully open and asked if she knew what it was.

"Oh no," she replied, "but I always keep it pulled out so that I can hang my handbag on it."

A Morning in Spring
Richard Jewel

Joyously greeting the new day just breaking
Blissfully happy this moment to fill
A Mighty Orchestry pure melody making
Which rolls on and on, over valley and hill.

"Good morning – I'm your new dawn chorus."

A MAN was travelling to Carlisle on a Scottish night express from London, and asked the guard to waken him at his destination.

"If you find it difficult," he told the guard jokingly, "just bundle me out bag and baggage."

He awoke just as the train was nearing Edinburgh, and in a rage sought out the guard to give him a piece of his mind. The guard, who was a Yorkshire lad, took the outburst calmly and at the end of the tirade remarked:

"Ah lad, thar't a good swearer, but thi canna swear like the chap I chucked out at Carlisle."

WHEN A railway service was initiated in a small country area of which the station was the terminus, an old inhabitant took a great deal of persuasion to take a trip. One day he made his decision and afterwards, when he was telling his friends about it, his story was as follows:

"I mek nowt o' thee trains. Onny road I've diddled t' railway company. I bowt a return ticket and walked back."

IN THE the early days of the Wensleydale Railway line, a man called for a parcel one day and was told by the station master:

"Go and look for it in my office. We're very busy at present. We've a train expected."

ONE MORNING a dalesman came rushing up to the ticket barrier just as the train was pulling out.

"Oh 'eck," he gasped as he handed his ticket to the inspector. "If I run shall I catch it?"

"Aye," was the reply. "Tha'll beat it. It's goin' to t' sidin'."

THE GENERAL ELECTION of 1918 was the first time that women had been allowed to vote. At the polling station an old daleswoman was told:

"Put your vote in the box."

She replied: "Nay lad it's tekken all these years to give t' womin t' vote. Der ye think I'd give it up nah. Thee keep the box. I's takin mine 'ome and steg it on't mantleshelf."

WITH A wicked grin Fred Trueman told the tale of a county match between Glamorgan and Yorkshire on a beautiful day. An old-age pensioner went along to pay his membership subscription and the secretary said:

"You would have thought more people would have turned up on such a lovely morning."

The old lad replied: "Don't worry it'll fill up after lunch."

"Why is this?" asked the secretary.

There was a grin as the pensioner said:

"It's half day at Pateley Bridge."

ALWAYS I have dreamed of a walking tour – of wandering over hill and dale as fancy led – resting at nightfall in lone farmhouses or wayside inns, and never has the opportunity come until now. At the age of sixty-six and after a spinal accident thirteen years ago, which has necessitated a bathchair the dream has come true.

My son and his wife, both experienced climbers, and real lovers of the Yorkshire Dales have pushed me in my bathchair for an eight-days tour; eight miles through the Dales, including the climb over Buttertubs Pass.

Our route was Richmond, Reeth, Muker over Buttertubs to Hawes, over Greenside Pass to Buckden, Starbottom, Kettlewell, the beautiful Kilnsey Crag and so to Burnsall. Then via Bolton Tower and Bolton Abbey and Nesfield to Ilkley and on to Askwith. Thence through Otley and Pool, we climbed Arthinton Bank and home to Leeds.

I would say to others who ride in bathchairs and those who push them:

"Go out and do likewise."

Mary Thorne

WHEN AN aged parishioner asked what hymns they had sung at church the previous Sunday, the vicar mentioned 'The rosy hues of early dawn'. The old man replied:

"Aye, that's a luvly hymn. Them rows of ewes at early morn – that'd be a grand sight."

A SMALL boy from a Dales farm was visiting his aunt in a Yorkshire town. As she summonsed him to the table prior to the beginning of the meal he eyed his side plate with misgivings.

"Surely you have plates at home," said his aunt.

"Aye we does," he replied, "but nut wi nowt on it."

"The best way to double your money is to fold it and put it back I'th' pocket."

FRED WAS always late turning up to work in a West Riding mill.

One morning the boss said:

"Nah then, Fred, dusta kna t' buzzer's gone?"

Said Fred without embarrassment:

"A'm nut surprised. The'll pinch owt these days."

A POLICEMAN in a Dales village knew old Sarah well. She was 'turned eighty' and her husband had died suddenly two years before. He was a man who had seen to everything and when he went Sarah couldn't cope on her own. She took to her bed and stayed there.

Everyone in the village rallied round, some did her shopping, some did her housework and the policeman took on the job of drawing her pension for her every week. Her house door was never locked; everyone went straight upstairs for a chat and a cup of tea, the makings of which she had in her bedroom.

She was nearly blind but could often recognise people by their voices. One day, however, the policeman was going into the house just as the doctor was leaving. He asked how she was. He said that there was nothing physically wrong with her and she could live to be a hundred. The policeman went up and spoke to her.

She said: "Has t' parson gone?"

"It wasn't t ' parson, Sarah; it was Doctor Wade."

A smile spread over her old face.

"Oh does tha kna, Ah thowt parson were gettin' a bit cheeky."

IN 1899, a knur and spell player called Joe Machin, who lived near Barnsley, hit a pot knur weighing half an ounce just over fifteen score yards (over 300 yards) – a feat that has never been surpassed.

These 'spells' are made of iron, with a spiked base for driving into the ground. A long, flat spring with a little brass cap at one end to hold the knur is held down by a trigger. The knurs are about the size of a big marble. The player taps the trigger with the end of his stick, and then hits at the knur as it is flung up by the spring.

Usually, each contestant is allowed thirty attempts, mis-hits counting. Sometimes the winner is the man who has walloped the knur the greatest distance with any hit. Sometimes all the distances are totalled. Another variation, once called 'poor man's golf' fixes a distance that has to be covered by the knur in the minimum number of strokes. For this game, the spell is moved forward after each knock.

The game was popular all over Yorkshire in the nineteenth century, but the men from Hunslet were famous for their skill in this sport. The sticks used by the men were about four feet long, most of them made of ash. One such was once a Leeds cabby's whip, "And it's ideal for this job," said player Eddie Thompson.

The knur is struck with a shaped block called the 'buck head' or 'pummel' fixed to the end of the stick. This is often made of beech faced with maple wood, but the Hunslet experts thought that maple was too soft and used only beech.

A few years ago, at Barkisland, near Halifax, there was

an attempt to revive knur and spell that eventually failed, because as one of the men put it:

"There's no interest amongst t' young 'uns and t' old laikers are past it."

THE STRENUOUS art of 'peak bagging' seems to have lost much of its attraction these days. There was never much to be said for the feat, for the joy of climbing peaks becomes thin if they are regarded as Mere Aunt Sallies to be bowled over.

Yet the surmounting of the three great hills of Whernside, Ingleborough and Penyghent, even though climbed on separate occasions, is something that should be done by all who love our Yorkshire hills. Each peak has its attractions, and the walker should allow sufficient time on each summit for their proper enjoyment.

There is no finer introduction to the Dales country than the ascent of these three noble hills.

THE VERGER, talking to a rector about a new visitor:

"I 'ope 'e'll be more pop'lar, like, than t' last one."

Then noticing on the visitor's face no expression of approval: "If that could possibly be, Sir."

A COMMERCIAL traveller, describing a little market town in which he had been immured for the weekend: "It was like Hell with the fire out."

The Road Home
Q Nicholas

T' lamp-leet dapples t' pooany's back:
An' glints on buckle an' ring;
Away beyond t' edge there's nowt bud black
Wheeare t' neet 'ides ivrything:
Bud, snug iv a lahtle word o' leet
T' trap rumbles dreamily on through t' neet.
Up 'ill, down deeale, till round a bend
A leet gleams far away:
An t' awd meeare, scentin' 'er journeys end
An' t' steeable an' t' rack of 'ay
Gives a loud whinny, that seeams ti mean:
"That's t' lamp iv oor parlour.
We're 'ooame ageean.

"I'm not kidding – she gossips worse than a man."

OLD MARY went round to the surgery but Doctor John – a local lad – was on holiday. The locum was a stranger from the south of England, and who asked her what the trouble was. May replied: "Ah've cum abate me seet."

"Get undressed behind that screen, and lie down on the couch," said the doctor.

After he had examined her carefully he told her to get dressed again and said:

"You will be pleased to know that there is nothing wrong with you."

Mary gave him a look of absolute disdain and replied:

"Sithee lad, if I'd known there were to be all this fuss ower a pair of glasses I'd nivver 'ave bothered to cum."

"That'll larn thi to drop litter here just afore t' Best-kept Village judges have been round."

AN OLD daleswoman was tending her cottage garden when a young couple approached. The amorous young man picked a rose from the garden and presented it to his sweetheart. The young lady saw the daleswoman looking at her and asked:

"What do you call this rose?"

In a flash came the reply:

"Some folks calls 'em *rosa alba* but I calls this one thievin'."

VERY FEW people know that Scarborough once had a tower – and furthermore it revolved. It was 150 feet high and was called the Warwick Revolving Tower opened on August Bank Holiday, 1898. Some 300 tons of steel were used in its construction and a gas engine provided the motive power for the fifteen-foot wide revolving platform which carried a small orchestra.

The Warwick Revolving Tower proved to be a novelty for some but an eyesore for others who considered that it spoiled the natural beauty of Castle Hill. In those circumstances Mr Albert Shuttleworth, a prominent local citizen, considered that he was performing a public duty when he bought this "iron cage to hold 200 gapers". The sole reason for his purchase was to demolish the tower and this began in 1907.

This was the sad end for yet another 'revolution'.

FARMER TO land worker returning tardily from an errand:

"Th'art the reet man to send for trouble; tha's bin so long upporth road."

SOUTH YORKSHIRE housewife, describing her next-door neighbour:

"She's as jealous as 'ell of 'er 'usband, an' Lord knows Ah've seen better things than 'im come out o' a piece o' cheese."

OLD JOE was telling a friend that his wife had finally nagged him into moving house after forty years in a tiny cottage.

"Aye we was arguin' all mornin' abaht what to call it. She says Cloister an' I says the Willows."

"Thowt the' said it were a council 'ouse," said the friend.

"It is. She says we'ed be cloister t' shop, cloister t' pub and cloister ter t' church. I says afore long willow t' rent, willow t' gas and willow all soarts."

NOT FAR from York is the village of Askham there lived a farmer named Swan. A visitor walking through the village met a lad tending some ducks.

"Whose ducks are these?" he asked.

"Them's Swans," was the reply.

The visitor laughed and said:

"Na then lad, stop pullin' me leg. We'er do you come from?"

"Askham," said the lad.

The visitor went away tapping his forehead.

OVERHEARD BY two schoolboys on a bus from Skipton to Gargrave. They were discussing homework and one boy asked his friend:

"What do you think 'out of sight, out of mind' means?"

The friend thought for a while and said:

"Invisible and insane."

It was said of one Dales grocer that he was so mean he'd nip a currant in two.

A DALESMAN met a farmer friend on the beach at Whitby and said to him:

"What 'art thou doin' 'ere lad?"

"Ah git wed yesterdi, tha' knas."

"Well we'ers thi wife. Isn't she on t' honeymoon wi' thee?"

"Oh noa, she's at 'ome looking arter t' pigs. Thi sees, she's been here afore."

43

A LEEDS vicar died and was on his way to Heaven. St Peter asked him where he came from and on being told he was from Yorkshire replied:

"You can come in – but we can't be messing around making Yorkshire pudding just for one."

A DALESMAN was walking down a lane during the war and he was stopped by a Land Girl who had both hands stuffed in her breeches pocket.

She said: "I say mister is this the way to Oldham?"

He replied: "Nay lass I don't reetly knaw; I wear braces on mine."

"I'm as happy as a lamb with two mothers."

SAID THE farmer about his poor-quality land:

"What my farm wants is a shower of rain every day and a shower of muck on Sundays."

ANCIENT GARDENER, on being asked how he kept his garden so immaculate:

"Ah allus worrks facin' backads, nut forrads – tha can see what tha's dun and nut what tha's yit to tackle."

"HOW DID the car accident happen?"

"My wife feel asleep in the back of the car."

THE LADY who has attracted attention to Knaresborough through the ages is Mother Shipton. Some chroniclers aver that she never existed; others are positive that she did. She is said to have been born near Knaresborough in 1488 in July and baptised by the Abbot of Beverley under the name of Ursula Sontheil.

"Her stature was larger than common, her body crooked, her face frightful, but her understanding extraordinary," wrote an ancient chronicler.

About the age of twenty-four she was courted by Toby Shipton (brave lad?), a builder from Skipton.

She made remarkable prophecies including a flying machine, a description of what could be regarded as a car, but she did get a few things wrong: she predicted the end of the world in 1881.

"You get off home, love. There's some queer characters abroad these nights."

Owd Ben's Advice
Dennis Page

A chap *hez nobbut once ta live*
He's nobbut once ta dee;
His days dahn 'ere are nobbut few
So 'earken lad ta me
Enjoy thissen well still tha'rt young
An' dunnot ape l'owd men;
Tha'll be grey and doitin' sooin enuff
Baht doin' it thissen.
Live thi lahf as best tha can
Be honest gooid an' streyt:
Then if tha follers this advayce
Tha'll get ta heaven all reyt.

A NEWLY married couple bought a cottage in the Dales. After they came back from a viewing, they remembered that they had not noticed the WC, so they wrote to the vicar who thought that 'WC' meant the Wesleyan chapel, and he replied:

Dear Sir:

I regret any delay in answering your letter but the WC is seven miles from your house. This is rather unfortunate if you are in the habit of going regularly. However, it might please you to know that some people take their lunch and make a day of it.

By the way it is made to hold 300 people and the committee decided to ensure greater comfort by installing plush seats. Those who can spare the time walk to it, whilst others take the train. I myself obviously never go but my wife went two years ago but she had to stand all the time.

PS: Hymn sheets will be found hanging behind the door.

I do hope this helps and hope you will be comfortable.

AN OLD farmer from Norland was waiting with his wife in a bus queue at Salterhebble near Halifax. The conductor shouted: "There's nobbut room for one."

The farmer dived in and shouted:

"Give us t' key lass and I'll hev t' kettle on when tha gets yam."

She had only four miles to walk.

OLD TRADITIONS die hard in the dales of Yorkshire. Many old Christmas customs that have disappeared in towns are still faithfully observed in the remote villages and hamlets.

Small girls tour houses and cottages with their wassail song as they have done for centuries past. They carry with them an oblong wooden box decked with cheap coloured muslin and ribbons, and containing a doll dressed up in gaudy clothes, surrounded by evergreens and paper flowers. With this humble analogy to the Holy Child they travel from door to door reciting a doggerel which dates back centuries:

> *Here we come a'wassailing*
> *Among the leaves so green*
> *Here we come a' wassailing*
> *So fair to be seen.*
> *Love and joy come to you*
> *And to you a wassail too*
> *And may God bless you and sen you*
> *God bless the master of the house*
> *The mistress also here.*
> *Love and joy come to you*
> *And to you a wassail too*
> *And God bless you, and send you*
> *A Happy New Year.*

Then they would knock on the door, and ask for sweets or pence.

JOHN WALTON was born in Bradford in 1817 but moved to Sutton-in-Craven with his widowed mother in the 1840s. He preferred to be called Painter Jack but his talent was questionable. He was, however, commissioned by a local chapel to paint a biblical scene. He produced a huge all-red canvas.

"What does that depict?" asked the puzzled cleric.

"It's Moses and t' Israelites crossin' t' red sea," said Jack.

"Well where are they?"

"The've nobbut just gitten across."

"Well where are the pursuers, the Egyptians?" persisted the cleric.

"They're under t' watter, drownded," explained Jack.

A LADY who kept a budgie thought it looked lonely and decided to buy it a mate. This she did, but in looking in the cage next morning she found the new bird dead. The old budgie looked very sprightly.

"All right," she said. "I'll teach you a lesson." She borrowed an owl from the local zoo and put it in the cage. Next morning the owl was dead and the budgie was looking very cheeky.

So the lady borrowed an eagle and put it in the cage. The next morning the eagle was dead. The budgie had lost all of its feathers.

"Oh dear," said the owner, "whatever has it done to you?"

The budgie replied:

"Oh I'm alright, but I had to tek mi jacket off to deal with that 'un."

One church service was interrupted when a young lad rushed in and shouted: "Daddy, nanny goat's gotten loose."

A DALESMAN was watching rooks building their nests.

"Dosta know rooks use only two types of twig?"

The townsman tried to guess.

"Are they ash, oak, birch, beach, alder or what?" he asked.

"None on 'em – t' rooks nobbut use bent 'uns an' straight 'uns."

"...and you only tweet when you're twoten to."

A POSTMAN in the Dales was seen running at top speed across a field by the road. He cleared a five-barred gate at a jump and picked himself up just as a frenzied bull charged the gate.

A passer-by said:

"That's a narrow escape you've had this morning."

"This morning?" said the postman, pulling bits of grass and nettle from his tunic. "This morning? It happens every morning."

A BRIDLINGTON fisherman was watching visitors pouring in from coaches and pouring down beer on a hot day. A couple of drunks approached the fisherman who was leaning on the harbour wall. The tide was out and a visitor asked: "We're'st watter gone?"

The reply came in a flash. "It were 'ere when tha cum. 'Appen tha's supped it all."

CUSTOMERS IN a shop in Hawes were interrupted by a lady obviously in a hurry who jumped the queue.

"Quick," she said. "Gimme a fly paper. I hev ter catch a train."

"Albert! Gentleman here with a tile loose."

MARTHA WOOD will be remembered as a confectioner in the old Haworth main street where she had lived all of her very long life. It was reported in the village that a new vicar was making a lot of changes to the church service.

Now the old 'Haworther' disliked change and seeing the vicar pass one morning, Martha called out:

"Ow vicar, come over 'ere."

He crossed the street.

"They tells me things are a bit different-like at church since the' commed. I'm tellin' thee nah tha can alter all t' hymn-tunes that tha likes, but I'll go on singin' em to t' old uns."

A LAD FROM Dent told of his childhood days in Cowgill on the outskirts of the village. Willie was a clogger, one of the essential jobs which meant that so many places were self sufficient. There were characters and skilled craftsmen aplenty.

"I sat up wi' owd Willie many a time. He were an owld chap wi' whiskers. Plenty of kids were freetened on 'im but I weren't. I used to take mi clogs to 'im but I got as I could put mi own caukers on. So I didn't see 'im as often, but I remember when he waved his whiskers wobbled as if there were a wind blowin'."

"MY SISTER and me," said a woman, "we ain't no more alike than if we wasn't us. Yes, she's just as different as me, only the other way."

The Cobbler

I started my life as a cobbler:
I cobbled from morn until night.
I've worked and I've strived for a living:
I've worked and I've cobbled all of my life.

Chorus
I'll soon have to put up mi shutters
The business is getting quite done.
I can't earn enough for me bacca
I think that my time is run.

A GOLFING parson badly beaten by an elderly pensioner, returned to the club house obviously depressed.

"Cheer up," said the old dalesman. "Tha'll be buryin' me soon."

"Yes," said the parson, "but even then it'll be your hole."

A QUAKER one day rode up to the home of the lady of his choice and, when she came to the door, said briefly:

"Rachael, the Lord has sent me to marry thee."

With equal brevity the lady at once replied:

"The Lord's will be done."

STRANGE EVENTS have been enacted at the Cow and Calf rocks, the fame of which is second only to the raucous ditty of *On Ilkla Moor Baht' 'at*, sometimes sung by those who may never have even heard of Yorkshire. There have been cavemen swarming all over the moor but visitors need not have worried because they were only filming an episode of *Monty Python's Flying Circus*.

IN THE 1930s the Silent Inn at Stanbury near Haworth was still a farm offering accommodation and home-brewed ale to visitors. It is said that when Bonnie Prince Charlie was fleeing from his enemies in 1745 this inn was one of his overnight stops. The pursuers nearly caught up with him but he managed to escape across a small bridge at the bottom of the hill.

All of the people in and around the inn were sworn to secrecy about the 'Bonny Prince' and hence the name of the Silent Inn.

SAID THE country butcher: "Ah fitted 'is mother with meat for five an' twenty years."

OLD GENTLEMAN at dinner, toasting the local MP:

"Politicians always remind me of a litter of pigs because those that have their snouts in the trough are very quiet but the ones left outside kick up a devil of a noise."

A SEVEN-YEAR-OLD flew from America to spend Christmas with her grandparents. Her daddy said:

"We came by Jumbo jet and every seat was occupied."

The little girl had her say and said:

"When I war right up there I looked everywhere for God but I couldn't see Him anywhere."

AFTER CHAPEL a member complained why the Methodist minister preached such a long sermon. His reply was:

"Listen 'ere lad. If tha' knew what I left aht, tha' wudd'na worrit abaht what I put in."

IN THE days before motor transport, a country parson who was leaving the district asked a Dales farmer how much he wanted for taking a load of furniture to the station.

"Nay," said the farmer, "Ah nivver charges nowt fer flittin' a parson. If 'e's a mon yer like, it's a pleasure to 'elp 'im. An' if 'es a mon ya deeant like, it's a pleasure to be rid on 'im."

BILLY WAS not a regular churchgoer. One day he met a martinet of a vicar.

"How is it you are not at church more often?" he asked.

"I've bin twice and were nut treated vera we-al at either," replied Billy.

"How do you mean?"

"First time they chucked watter o'er mi 'ed; and t' second time they tied a woman ter mi shirt tails."

"Well," said the vicar, "the worst is over. You can come to church in safety."

"Nay," Billy asserted. "Ah nahs there hes to be a next time, but nut yet vicar – nut yet."

"T' trouble wi' some folk who have more money than brains is that they haven't gitten much money either."

THE BIG puzzle about the Puzzle Hall Inn in Sowerby Bridge is how it got its name. It's likely to be as simple as the look of the place with its many sloping roofs. Or a reference to a maze between the inn and the river Calder. The pub did have boats for hire before the war, stairs under a courtyard supposedly connecting the pub to the river.

The early seventeenth century building was a private dwelling for a hundred years before becoming a pub. In 1860 its licensee John Luty was fined thirty shillings for allowing tossing (gambling on the fall of a coin).

John Platt, husband of Lydia Marsh whose father was a former landlord, established a brewery there around 1895. Platt died in 1912 when he fell off the roof while carrying out repairs. Wards of Sheffield bought the pub and closed the brewery in 1935, and up to the 1950s beer supplies arrived by train.

Today the Puzzle is a lively music venue.

A MAN in the village was puffing and blowing as he pushed a heavily laden wheelbarrow up a slight incline. Coming up behind, a small boy shouted: "Hey, mister, Ah'll grunt for thi – thee 'od thi breath an' push."

PUZZLING FOR a long time over an official form, the roadman, who had lost a leg, finally entered his occupation as 'wooden-legged highwayman'.

Broth and Dumplings

Doris Shepherd

Flagged floors, black lead
Side ovens, home-baked bread.
Chip shops with sanded floors
Iron snecks to fasten doors.
Oil lamps burning bright
Knocker-up, early light.
Suet dumplings, hot broth
Field days, coffee and bun
Maypole dancers having fun.
Top and whip, shuttlecocks
Knickerbockers, cotton frocks
Cashmere shawls, long skirts.
Gradely folks, days of old
Friendly folks with hearts of gold.

IN A juvenile court a boy of nine came to give evidence on behalf of his elder brother, who was charged with an offence. The chairman asked kindly:

"Now then Michael – do you know what happens if a boy promises in court to tell the truth and then tells lies?"

He replied in a flash.

"Yes sir – he gets off."

IN 1759, A Mr Courtney of Beverley wished to send £2,000 to London for investments and he at once faced a problem that would not exist today: that of sending money to his London broker. Without bankers there were no cheques, and to send such a sum in cash by a stagecoach was a hazardous enterprise as it would have been tempting to the footpads and highwaymen.

Mr Courtney arranged to buy some bills of exchange from Mr Dixon of Leeds, who sent two representatives to the Black Swan at York where a message summoned them to go on to Beverley. Thus, before they returned to Leeds they would cover about a hundred miles on horseback over indifferent roads. Reaching Beverley the coins had to be counted and separately weighed, and the checking of his comparatively small sum occupied them for two and a quarter hours.

ELDERLY VISITOR, asked if he would like the electric fire switched on:

"Nay, nay, I'm nown cauld; I'm warm as two puddens."

ELDERLY SCARBOROUGH fisherman sat on the pier watching with disfavour the noisy water-skiers tearing up and down near the harbour until their sport was halted by engine failure:

"Aye, well, that'll take the steam out of their sails."

IN THE days of thick smog, a lorry trawled slowly along on the road towards Hull. His mate was at the front shining a torch. Then the fog lifted a little and the driver shouted:

"Al reet, Fred – tha can git in nah."

A surprised voice shouted back:

"Eye up, lad, my name's nut Fred."

CHARLIE HAD a farm which was the muckiest in the whole of England. You needed only two requirements when visiting Charlie – a pair of wellies and a shovel. All around his farmyard was muck. Every time the cows came in for milking they paddled and slushed their way through mud. One day a gamekeeper arrived to shoot rabbits. He jumped into his Land Rover and sank. The next step he took was in his stockinged feet, for his wellies were implanted in the muck. His spaniel took one look at the mess and jumped back into the Land Rover. As the gamekeeper beat a hasty retreat, the postman rode into the yard on his bicycle and became stuck in the muck. The postie and his letters became splashed in the evil-smelling mess.

One day Charlie went to the market to sell some pigs which were crowded into his equally mucky vehicle. When the animals were being unloaded the auctioneer said: "Ah didn't kna that kept Bilsdale blues, Charlie."

"Thems not Bilsdale Blues," was the reply. "Them is large whites."

A SCHOOLMISTRESS asked a pupil: "What tree grows from a conker?"

There was no reply and so she said:

"It's a horse chestnut. I wonder why they call them conkers?"

This time there was a response.

"It musta bin named after somebody. It were William the Conker."

The schoolmistress discovered that the old name for a snail shell was 'conquer' and the game used to be played using the shells.

The Farm Cat

Q Nicholas

T' leeak at
T' awd tom cat
Isn't what thoo'd call bonny.
Neea knawn breeäd
Ugly 'eead
Cooa't a sheeäde ower monny.
Rough I' t' fur
Dizzn't purr
Strooäke 'im an' 'e'll walk away
Ya leg leeäme
Pooächin' geeäme
'E got it iv a trap ya day

Aye, 'e's not
Worth a lot:
But what diz sike-like matter?
Though 'e's pleeän:
When all's deeän
t' awl lad's a champion ratter

THE EXTENDED use of wheeled carriages, goods wagons and stagecoaches made many of the older roads unsuitable because of their steep gradients, so that new lines of roads had to be laid out. This involved surveying the proposed routes and determining levels, and surveying the ground for the purchase of land along the route.

The most spectacular Yorkshire figure in this connection is that of Blind Jack, to whose skill we owe many hundreds of miles of roads still in use in the county. Although Jack never made a map, he surveyed the line for many roads.

John Metcalfe was born at Knaresborough on the 15th August 1717, and was a normal child until the age of six years, when a bout of smallpox left him totally blind. He seems to have been a clever and courageous lad, and soon learned to find his way alone anywhere around Knaresborough, and managed to join and lead other boys in their games and pranks. He seemed to suffer very little disability from his blindness and his life story is a better read than almost any novel.

His direct connection with roads begins in 1751 when he set up a stage-wagon service between Knaresborough to York, running twice a week in summer and weekly in winter, until such time as he took his first road-making contract. This was the three miles between Minskip and Fearnsby on the first turnpike authorised from Harrogate to Boroughbridge. This he followed by building a bridge with an 18-foot span at Boroughbridge and by contracting for a road between Knaresborough and Harrogate. Other road contracts followed in rapid succession, including portions of the turnpikes between Skipton and Colne, Chapeltown and Leeds, Halifax and Wakefield and many others. Metcalfe made his surveys and estimates on a method entirely his own, but evidently one which was very reliable and efficient.

He surveyed and traversed all the ground, used his staff as a sounding rod, felt the materials, and laid out some excellent lines on good foundations.

He was one of the first road-makers to build safely on boggy ground, and both his roads and bridges remain to this day monuments to the skill and accuracy of his surveying.

WHEN THE little evacuee to the Yorkshire Dales first heard a cow, he raced to the farmhouse in fear, and panted: "The big cow blew one of her horns like anything."

IN THE nursery the little girl pondered: "It is wretched being a girl when one has made no lady-plans and all one's boy-plans have crashed."

AGED SEXTON to equally aged colonel in a Wolds churchyard:

"I don't want to hurry you, sir, but you'd best pick your bit or all t' best places will be took."

THE ALICE Hawthorn Inn at Nun Munkton, York, was named after the famous racehorse which ran in seventy-one races, won fifty-one of them, and was placed ten times. Between 1842 and 1845 she won sixteen cups, including the Doncaster, Goodwood, Chester, the Queen's Vase and eighteen Queen's Plates.

When her racing days were finished, she became one of the greatest brood mares in racing history. She is said to have been named after the owner's beautiful mistress. There is another Alice Hawthorn Inn at Wheldrake, between York and Selby

WHEN A London couple bought a certain inn on the North York Moors in the 1960s they decided to take it upmarket, serving hot food and selling bottles of wine. They hoped that, with a little training, Maggie, the barmaid from the local village, would be as popular in the restaurant as she was in the bar.

The squire and his lady thought they should try the new enterprise.

"I hear you sell wine, Maggie," said Sir Henry.

"Oh, yes sir," said Maggie proudly. "There's red or white and it's two guineas a bottle."

"Do you have rosé?" asked M'Lady.

"Oh yes, madam, but it'll be four guineas as we'll 'ave to oppen two bottles."

"Kissing don't last; cookery do!"

"Make that the last trump, Gabriel; supper's ready."

A YOUNG couple in Harrogate did very well in their married life until the wife acquired and became enthusiastic about a cookery book on how to use up left-overs. Although the husband always asked a blessing before each meal, one day he merely lifted the lid of the dish and then replaced it.

"Why don't you ask a blessing?" enquired his wife.

"I reckon everything in that dish has already been blessed six times," replied hubby.

THE WI had just sat through a lecture on the subject of healthy eating. They had been exhorted to adopt a vegetarian diet, to abandon saturated fats and refined flour, and to embrace the ideal of wholemeal and high fibre. In addition they were told that the practice of yoga and transcendental meditation would transform their lives. At this point a member on the back row put up her hand.

"Can tha do thowt transference as well as yon yodurt and transatlantic medication?" she asked.

Modestly the speaker admitted to some small skill which she occasionally exercised.

"Well tha' should have exercised it today," said the member of the back row. "Ah've just med thee a ham sandwich wi' white bread."

"I've no radiogram, but the BBC have played 3,271 of my record requests."

AN OLD lady living in a remote Dales village was paying her second visit to a doctor in Harrogate and hailed the busy service bus. She held out her fare and looked up into the conductor's face and said: "Please will you put me down at the same place as last month?"

A NEWCOMER to the Dales was travelling by bus and was spoken to by the conductor. She explained that she was on the bus because her husband had the car. The conductor asked for details of the car. When asked why the reply was: "Well, we know thee now and if we push any car into ditch on these narrow roads we'd rather it were somebody we don't know."

A DALESMAN was enjoying his usual pint when his friend limped in.

"Whats tha limpin' fower?"

"It's mi veins – they'r too close together."

"Who told thi that?"

"Mi doctor – 'e sez I've got very close veins."

A COUPLE of old dalesmen were discussing even older folk.

"My uncle is ninety-two and he's nobbut just stopped ridin' 'is bike."

The other even older chap quickly responded.

"Wots up? 'As ee 'ad a puncture?"

THERE IS Good Friday, Shrove Tuesday and Ash Wednesday. But what about Collop Monday? Few people know of this annual event which is still celebrated in at least one pocket of West Yorkshire – at Meltham near Huddersfield.

It falls on the Monday before Ash Wednesday when the forty-day fast of Lent begins. Centuries ago the fast was rigidly observed in England so, just before the famine – so to speak – a feast was held. A country family would kill a pig and prepare collops – round, flat, pieces of bacon, which would be eaten on Collop Monday. Any surplus meat would be given away.

The tradition slowly changed and, instead of providing collops of meat, sweets were given to children and even the shopkeepers of Meltham joined in. In more mercenary times coins replaced the sweets.

TWO WOMAN, meeting one another in London:

"Ah believe we coom fra t' same parts. Ah'm Lancashire."

"Eh well, Ah'm fra' Yorkshire, but it's too 'ot to squabble now."

SAID A woman in the 1930s who had just moved into a new council house in Doncaster:

"Come and look at mi scullery – I get water out of a tap."

A DALESMAN took his son to a posh school in the south of England and said to the headmaster:

"Nah then, headmaister, Ah wont me son to talk like thee."

The headmaster said that it would be difficult unless he left the boy at the school for two years without coming home. After two years the dalesman came to collect his son. He asked the headmaster for progress and the teacher replied:

"If tha' leaves t' lad another year, I think I can do summat wi' him."

"No 24 – Bellyache."

THE POMPOUS incumbent of a large north-country parish was far from popular. It was therefore without regrets that his two assistants found themselves being promoted to being vicar and curate of a small town a few miles away. The Sunday before his departure, the elder of the two assistants preached to a packed congregation. He took as his text the words from Genesis chapter 22 verse 5:

"Abide ye here with the ass; and I and the lad will go yonder and worship."

A SEXTON in a Dales village was digging a grave. It was well away from all the others in the churchyard. A visitor approached the sexton and asked him why the plot was so far from the others.

The reply was:

"Well a nah he's nobbut lived 'ere for twelve years and this is we'ere I puts oddments."

A DALES grocer thought he was being cheated. He bought his butter from a local farmer and was convinced he was being given short measure. One day when he called to deliver groceries and collect his butter he said to the farmer.

"How does thou weigh thi butter?"

Came the reply:

"I weighs it wi' thi sugar."

The Bandy-legged Sheepdog

A bandy-legged sheepdog of Hawes
Got some frozen meat wedged in its jaws.
They sent for the vet,
Who said: "Do nothing yet:
Just wait till the obstruction thaws."

A bandy-legged sheepdog of Hawes
Said: "My legs don't keep to the laws:
I wobble left and right
Which is awkward at night:
As I can't even follow my nose."

"It's about the rising damp…"

A DALESMAN was roused at night by the local doctor, who reported that there was a blockage in his toilet. The plumber protested about the lateness of the hour, but the doctor was adamant that something should be done about it immediately. The plumber arrived at the doctor's house, and with the doctor looked at the blocked toilet. The plumber said:

"I'll chuck an asprin dahn t' pan and we'll see 'ow it is in t' mornin'."

TWO DALES families were having an argument over who owned a wall between their properties. One went to a solicitor who said:

"I'm sorry I can't act for you because your neighbour has already briefed me. However, I can give you a letter to take to another solicitor in town."

Wondering why a letter was needed, the householder opened the letter which read:

"Here are two birds ripe for plucking. You pluck one and I'll pluck the other."

The neighbours settled their dispute and were friends who lived happily thereafter.

"Has ta ever noticed that brass tha owes is allus more than tha' reckoned, and t' brass owed to thee is allus less than tha thowt?"

OLD BILL liked his ale, but on returning home after a 'session' he was always on the receiving end of his wife's whiplash tongue. One night he decided to give her a fright. He went upstairs, painted his face with flour and lay on the bed as if dead. On seeing him his wife said:

"By gum Bill, tha' looks better deead then ivver that did when tha wor alive."

Bill jumped up and retorted:

"Well if that's all tha' thinks abaht me, Ah'll never dee agean as long as Ah lives."

WE ALL know of *Old Moore's Almanac* but who was Old Moore? Was he a real person, people ask as they buy their annual copy?

His real name was Albert Walker, and his father, William, started a printing company in Otley which became a limited company in 1904. Eventually the firm owned a group of newspapers consisting of *The Wharfedale and Airedale Observer*, *The Ilkley Free Press and Gazette* and *The Shipley Times and Express*.

A copy of *The Road*, or *Leaves from the Sketch Book of a Commercial Traveller*, which Albert Walker wrote in the 1920s, was signed for a friend:

"To Davy Holroyd with Compliments and Kind-est Wishes from the Author known as 'Old Moore' but in private as Albert Walker. In token and remembered of a very enjoyable evening which he spent at his residence on Saturday Jan 7 1922 and then on the verge of his 82nd year."

OVERHEARD AT the livestock ring of a country show:

"I shouldn't think never such a thing hasn't happened never before, not to win two cups."

GARDENER, RUEFULLY surveying weedy border: "There in't nobody what wouldn't think that 'ere bed 'adn't bin wed last week."

TWO DALES shopkeepers were debating the subject of economy. One asked:

"How's business?"

The reply came quickly.

"Terrible. Even them that don't intend payin' aren't buying owt."

A MAN was seen coming out of a house carrying a steaming kettle.

"Hello," said a friend. "Ah thowt tha'd flitted from that house."

"Aye," said the other. "We flitted last neet, but t' penny worn't done in t' gas so Ah've been boilin' t' kettle theer."

A FARMER in the Dales had been told by his doctor to take a holiday by the sea, and despite many objections he had at last gone to the west coast for the first time in his life. One day he was leaning over the rails of the promenade admiring the view. It was bright and sunny with a clear view for miles up the coast and over the sea to the horizon. A holidaymaker near him remarked on the extensive vista spread out before them.

"Aye," answered the farmer, "it's o'reet but if yon sea were nobbut jus' grass, wot a great load o' sheep you could git on it."

A DALES doctor returned from his afternoon rounds on a darkening winter's day. A message awaited him to say that the occupant of an isolated farm was "feelin queer, like, and could not eat nor breathe proper like cus 'is throat's blocked". The doctor walked the nine miles and when he knocked the bedroom window was opened. The farmer shouted:

"I nivver thowt tha' thowd come at this time o' neet. I's reet nah but wham un I do if mi throat gits closed up ageean?"

The doctor with a wry smile on his face shouted back: "Cut it."

FOR WHOOPING cough in children, onions were placed between alternate layers of brown sugar in a basin. After being allowed to stand overnight, the mixture was given in teaspoonfuls every three hours and was said never to have failed. Coltsfoot and tallow in the form of an embrocation was rubbed on the chests of miners as a precaution against lung diseases.

IN A BRADFORD school a teacher had been talking to her class about the history of Russia. She explained that the rulers were the Tsars and some were good and some were bad. The Tsar's wife was called the Tsarina. At this point a voice was heard:

"Were their children called Tsardines?"

A farmer knocked on the pearly gate,
His face was scarred and old;
He stood before the man of fate
For admission to the fold.
"What have you done?" St Peter asked:
"To gain admission here?"
"I've been a farmer, sir," he said
"For many and many a year."
The pearly gate swung open wide
As St Peter touched the bell.
"Come in," he said, "and choose your harp…
"You've had your taste of Hell."

"What a lot o' time folk waste trying to go places in a hurry."

AN ELDERLY daleswoman carefully climbed onto the bus and asked the driver to go steadily as she was going to the infirmary. At the stop the conductor helped her off the bus and asked if all was well. The old lady replied:

"I jus' med a jelly to tek to t' infirmary and it hadn't quite set when I left oahm."

A YORKSHIRE miner was having trouble getting his teenage son up in time to join him on the early shift. One morning the father decided to make certain of getting his son up in time for work. He sat down on the end of the bed. The son got up and went to work.

"Whose gitten thee up this morning?" asked the boss.

"Mi father," replied the lad.

"But where's thi father?" said the boss.

"I don't know," came the reply. "But he wor asleep at the end o' mi bed when I gorrup."

YEARS AGO, when a new railway line was being made up the Worth Valley, there was much competition among local men for jobs as porters. As the line was nearing completion, the village men thought they would get in some practice. Walking through the village at night a stranger might have been puzzled to hear the clang of an oven door closing and a loud voice shouting:

"All change. All change."

YORKSHIRE FOLK have always been noted for their faith in herbs. Many of our present-day remedies originated in the isolated farmhouses and cottages in the Dales. A few years ago an old farmer who lived high up on the fell above Ingleton was asked how the villagers had fared in the recent influenza epidemic. He remarked with obvious pride:

"We don't hold much wi' t' doctors up here. We gather all t' herbs we want. One day in't winter I had it bad so t' missus tummed me wi' elderflowers and t' next mornin' I wor feightin' fit. No doctor's medicine could do that for thee."

At certain times of the year, folk would be seen combing the fields and hedgerows in search of herbs which they took home and made into salves, oils, decoctions and infusions. Angelica for colds and coughs, balm for nervous headaches, broom for kidney complaints, hops for nervous disorders. Groundsel was once called 'the sickle plant' on account of its effectiveness, when used in poultices, against cuts caused during harvesting. Hops were used to treat nervous disorders which is perhaps why a drunk has few worries…

Wartime memories: "We ate leftovers so often that I don't even remember the original meal."

"When the driver's missed a necessary turning, gently tap his left shoulder, adopt a quiet but authoritative tone of voice and say..."

A MOTORIST had just crashed into a telephone pole – wires, pole, everything came down over his ears. As rescuers untangled him from the wreckage, he reached out feebly, fingered the wires and murmured:

"Thank God I lived clean. They've given me a harp."

IF MY body was a car I would be trading it in for a newer model. I've got bumps, dents, scratches and my head-lights are out of focus. My gearbox keeps seizing up and it takes me hours to reach maximum speed. I overheat for no reason and every time I sneeze, cough or laugh either my radiator leaks or my exhaust backfires.

A DALES shepherd with his shepherd's crook hanging on a hook on the wall was visited by a town-based official sent to assess the value of his cottage. On being asked where the toilet was, he took him down the garden and pointed to the privy.

"Gracious me," said the official, "there is no lock on the door."

"Don't thee fret abaht that. I've lived here for fifty years and nobody's ever pinched t' bucket."

AN ELDERLY daleswoman in a great state of agitation rushed into the post office and handed a key to the postmistress.

"My husband's just gone by train and forgotten to take the key to his suitcase," she said. "Can you get it to him quickly?"

The postmistress advised her to wrap it up and post it immediately but the old lass would have none of it.

"He must have it straight away," she said. "I want it telegraphed."

AN OLD dalesman got into a crowded train and placed a dripping box on the luggage rack. The drops began to fall on the bald head of a posh man from the city.

"Would you mind moving the rain water from the box – it's falling on my head," said the posh man.

The dalesman got up and moved the box, replying:

"That's nut rain – it's nobbut mi young pup."

"Love of brass is t' root of half t' world's troubles, and lack of brass is t' root of t' other half."

SAID BILL to Bob as they were walking to work early in the morning:

"Tha saands to heve a pocketful 'o brass."

"Brass be blowed," said Bill. "It's wife's false teeth. There's far too much etten between meals at ahr house when I'm not theer."

TWO DALESMEN were looking at a helicopter hovering above a reservoir.

"How longs yon thing bin hoverin' up thear?"

"Nigh on an hour," was the reply.

"Dusta reckon it's run aht o' petrol?"

MANY YEARS ago an assistant in a chemist's shop in a Yorkshire town where life was a bit rough was asked by a woman to treat a badly discoloured eye.

She said there had been "a bit of a fight at our house" and that she had been struck.

The assistant said politely that he hoped it was not her husband.

"Mi 'usband?" she said. "Nay, he didn't do it. Why he's more of a friend than a husband."

There's nivver nowt but what there's summat:
And when there's summat it's often nowt;
An them that allus think thev summat
Has nearly allus risen from nowt.
It's no use sittin' an' waitin' for summat:
For more often it nobbut ends wi' nowt –
And come to think on it, these lines I've penned
Are mainly summat abaht nowt.

"*As a ploughman I talks to mi horse, but when we gets a tractor, an' I talks to that, thee puts mi in here.*"

OVERHEARD IN a Yorkshire market. An old lady had bought a pack of four toilet rolls on a stall and was now bringing them back and demanding a refund.

"Whats wrong with 'em?" she was asked.

"Nowt," came the reply, "but the posh folk what was comin' nivver turned up and we can't afford to use stuff like this oursens."

ANOTHER OF Sar' Ann's children had just left school and started to work. Uncle Eli called.

"Well," he said, "an' how does ta feel now tha's getten another pullet layin'?"

A WEDDING which had taken place at a Yorkshire seaside resort was over. Bride and groom had gone off on their honeymoon, and a lady friend of the couple, who had been in charge of the arrangements, began to clear up.

Presents brought by the guests had been deposited in the cloakroom of the restaurant and the lady had never seen such a pile of lovely large parcels at any wedding. Surely the bride would never have to buy any bed linen again. Then she spent a long time packing the parcels into her small car which was crammed to capacity.

But just as she was about to drive away she was stopped and it was pointed out to her that those surprise packages contained a week's clean laundry for the restaurant.

BLEA MOOR Tunnel impresses a visitor by its splendid isolation, and by the height of its ventilation shafts. It is not a conspicuously dirty tunnel, though moisture and sulphur play such havoc with the track that it is replaced every four or five years. The normal life of a track in the open air is twenty-odd years.

Also impressive was the cheerfulness and skill of the railwaymen, who daily inspect the track, carry out repairs and re-line the tunnel. One of them remarked:

"Tha's bin lucky today. Tho'ull nobbut need a wesh when tha' gits home. Most days us needs a bath – aye, an' we've to change t' water several times an' all."

"I HEAR you're thinking o' keeping monkeys," said a Dales villager to the parson.

"Monkeys!" exclaimed the parson. "I never thought of such a thing."

Later it occurred to the reverend gentleman that a few days earlier he had approached the local landowner with a view to getting a better site for his apiary.

TWO VENERABLE gardeners were talking about the new owner's garden.

Said old George: "People who've got a garden and won't dig oughtn't to be allowed to eat vegetables."

Replied old Jim: "Bless you, they don't eat vegetables; they're vegetarians and has all their food out o' tins."

TWO ELDERLY dalesmen in Leyburn market-place were discussing the serious ailment of a third.

"Aye," said one. "Ah reckon only a post-mortem will show what it is."

"Maybe," replied the other. "But he's so weak he'd never stand that."

SOME TIME ago in a West Riding town a visitor was surprised to see near an old house a ha-ha and a gazebo within a short distance of each other. He mentioned this to a local looking over his fence. His reply was:

"Nay lad, tha's not reet. I've lived 'ere for nigh on seventy year and I've nivver sin two birds like those."

"It beats me what men find to talk about."

A YOUNG doctor from the south of England arrived to a practice in Skipton. He looked at a young lad whose mother told the doctor that "He were aht o' sorts".

"Put out your tongue," said the doctor but there was no response.

The lad's mother solved the problem.

"Oppen thi gob an' stick aht thi' lollicker."

This did the trick.

AN ECONOMIC crisis gives point to the story of the young husband pacing the floor of the waiting room at a Yorkshire maternity hospital when a smiling nurse entered:

"You are the father of triplets. You may come and see them and choose the one you will keep."

"Only one?" exclaimed the proud father. "Can't we keep all three."

"Under the present government," the nurse explained, "one is for you and two for export."

A GIRL from a Yorkshire village, on holiday in Leeds, saw an old man stumbling among the uprooted flag-stones on a road repairs site. She seized him firmly by the arm and led him past the scene of the excavations to safety. Then, when she asked him if he would be all right, he said:

"It's very kind of you to help me, my dear, but I must go back now – you see, I'm the nightwatchman."

A SMALL child and her grandparent were walking by a stream looking for water voles, which the youngster missed.

Suddenly she said: "Look at that big shell."

The grandparent looked, but could't see any shells until she realised the child meant a corrugated dustbin lid caught between stones.

LOOKING OUT of the window of his 'local' the farm man commented:

"By gum, yon horse has so many good points you could hang your hat on 'em."

"Twenty-one years working at Sharlston Colliery, and you break your wrist opening our coalhouse door."

AT AN agricultural meeting in Yorkshire there was concern because of a shortage of milk in one area. One of the members who felt strongly that this should be remedied, got on to his feet, and in loud tones addressed the meeting. "Gentlemen," he began, "we must take the bull by the horns and get the milk…"

WHEN JOE from the Dales was celebrating his eightieth birthday with a party, a newspaper reporter asked him what was his recipe for so long a life.

"Contentment," said Joe.

"So you have had a contented and happy life," said the reporter. "No domestic troubles?"

"No," said Joe. "When t' wife starts to natter I goes inter t' garden. If Ah'm wrong side out she goes inter t' kitchen."

"Well," said the reporter, "you look well."

"Yes," said Joe. "I spend a lot of time in t' garden."

Too much junk food will always go to waist.

SOME YEARS ago a man came across two small boys in a Craven village street. One was shaking the other unmercifully. "Why are you doing that?" the man asked, intending to part them.

"Well, you see, Ah found him drinking his medicine out o' t' bottle and on t' front it said 'Shake well'."

A Yorkshire Portrait

W Knowles

This county's one o' t' muckiest:
Wi' chimleys and belchin' smoke:
An' muck on slats on t' winders
An' steel and coal and coke.
Ha' can't escape from t' muck.
Most people there are cheery,
'ospitable and kind:
But some are reet tight-fisted, like:
Plenty o' them you'll find.
But if tha' gangs in t' country
Tha'll like the sights tha' sees
There nowt nowhere to beat it –
Hills, valleys, fields and trees.
Gi' me Yorkshire any day:
And if by word o' mouth
Tha sez that doesn't like it
Then get thesen down south.

Think of Yorkshire, hill and dale.
Moorland thrills that never pale.
Places where you've sat
On Ilkley Moor Baht 'at.
Sheffield steel so strong and true:
Woollen mills and foundries, too.
By gum how memories cling
And make you want to sing.

Chorus
Now here's a song for you and me:
There's no place like Yorkshire
Without a doubt you'll all agree
There's no place like Yorkshire
Some folks thinks we're maniacs
From Bradford, Leeds or Halifax:
Because we sing with open clacks
There's no place like Yorkshire.

MANY YEARS ago when the children at Askrigg prepared to start a game that required one particular individual to take some important part, they used this counting-out rhyme.

> "Oakum, bocum, stony cokum,
> Ellerkin, bellerkin, bony bush,
> Out goes he."
> Another version was:
> "Ipsy, dipsy, toodle ipsy;
> Allerber amber, toodle amber;
> Om, tom, tee, toe, tie, tosh,
> Out goes he."

A FRIEND'S tame owl flew into a lady's cottage at dusk and settled on the old lady's shoulder. Turning and seeing the wings above her, she cried: "My God, the angels have come for me!"

YORKSHIRE FARMER at village cricket match, seeing his pet lamb in the way of the ball:

"Arthur! Tek yon mucky tup out o' t' rooad; 'e'll be gerren 'issen 'itten else."

FARMER'S SON, asked if he had liked his first day at school:

"No, and I'm not going back – it's all office work."

THE CHILDREN had all been photographed, and the teacher was trying to persuade them each to buy a copy of the group picture.

"Just think how nice it will be to look at it when you are all grown up and say: 'There's Jennifer, she's a lawyer,' or 'That's Michael, he's a doctor.' "

A small voice at the back of the room rang out: "And there's the teacher, she's dead."

CHILDREN IN a Yorkshire school were having a knitting lesson when a small girl gave the teacher a tangle of wool and said: "Please unmuggle this."

"Actually – you'll be learning on something smaller."

A DALES farmer being asked one morning what the weather would be replied:

"Well it'ill happen donk and dozzle a bit and mebbe a flister or two, but there'll be nae gret pells."

A DALES farmer visited Leeds with his son whom he proposed to instruct in the ways of the great city. The first lesson took place as soon as they got outside the station. The farmer rapped hard on the pavement with his stick and then looked meaningfully at his son.

"Now you know why they have towns," he said. "Ground's too hard to plough."

LIKE SO many towns and cities which make brass and created muck during the Industrial Revolution, Leeds is proud of its town hall but is everything o' reet?

When its foundation stone was laid on 1st January 1855, things did not go smoothly. Nevertheless, Queen Victoria visited the building in 1858. There were plinths on each side of the colonnaded entrance. These looked bare until two sculptured white lions were set upon them. These soon became black with industrial soot and there were even objections when they were cleaned.

Perhaps this was to avoid them "freetening folk" because it was said they roamed about the square on New Year's Eve.

LITTLE GIRL, looking at rabbits: "Oh mummy, how funny – the rabbit winked its nose at me."

COALMINER, COMMENTING on his workmate's balding head: "No need to thatch an empty barn, eh George?"

George: "No, an' grass dun't grow in a busy street, neither."

FARMER TO worker: "How long will it take you to finish building that wall?"

Worker: "Well, gaffer, I reckon I done the biggest half; the rest on it will tek me the best part of some time."

AT A gathering near Bradford a workman was asked what a 'woolman' was. The reply was:

"He's a chap that buys wool at £2 a pound, sells it at £1.80 a pound and when he dies he leaves £750,000."

AN OUT-OF-TOWNER drove his car into a ditch in a desolated area. Luckily, a local farmer came to help with his big strong horse named Buddy.

He hitched Buddy up to the car and yelled: "Pull, Nellie, pull." Buddy didn't move.

Then the farmer hollered: "Pull, Buster, pull." Buddy didn't respond.

Once more the farmer commanded: "Pull, Jennie, pull." Nothing.

Then the farmer nonchalantly said: "Pull, Buddy, pull." And the horse easily dragged the car out of the ditch.

The motorist was most appreciative and very curious. He asked the farmer why he called his horse by the wrong name three times.

The farmer said: "Oh, Buddy is blind, and if he thought he was the only one pulling, he wouldn't even try!"

OVERHEARD IN a Skipton pub:

"Ee lad, but tha's gitten a big nose."

"Aye, but Ah once met a man wi'out yan and I've been grateful for mine ivver sin."

Sing As You Drive

At 45 mph sing: Highways are Happy Ways.
At 55 mph sing: I'm a Stranger but I'm Here,
Heaven in My Home.
At 65 mph sing: Nearer My God to Thee.
At 75 mph sing: When the Roll is Called up
Yonder, I'll Be There.
At 85 mph sing: Lord I'm Coming Home.

NOTING THE success of the Bradford Exhibition held in Lister Park during the summer of 1904 and closely followed by the White City exhibition in London, a group of Yorkshire businessmen in 1908 decided that there was a vast potential patronage for a West Riding zoo and amusement park.

Early in 1909 a limited company was formed, backed by a working capital of £17,000 to provide "the most up-to-date zoo and amusement park in England".

The site chosen for the new project was Chevin Edge at the top of Exley Bank, less than two miles from the centre of Halifax. Another reason was that a Mrs Davis was running tea rooms very successfully in the old mansion there. The open fields and woods round Exley made it an ideal location for this kind of venture.

At Whitsuntide 1909, the Halifax Zoo and Amusement Park opened with a flourish. The company were proud to present a collection of nearly a thousand animals, birds and reptiles. All the creatures were housed in new glazed houses and cages. There were lions and tigers, a llama, a zebra and a fully grown elephant was available to give rides to the kiddies.

On the north side of the mansion a portion of woods was cordoned off as a deer park and inside the main zoo seals and sealions besported themselves in a sunken tank. There was a spacious aviary and a miniature railway encircled the site. There was also a large area devoted to a roller skating rink, 'exiting rides' and a number of amusement arcades.

Until the onset of the 1914-18 war, Halifax Zoo was one

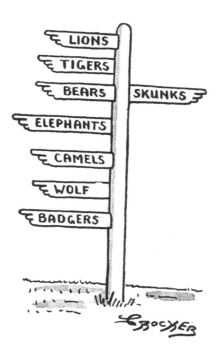

of the most popular venues in Yorkshire but in 1915 most of the animals were removed to places like Belle Vue in Manchester. The facility never really recovered but there was a brief revival in the 1920s when Halifax Town Football Club took over the site. Town were then in the Midland League but they later moved to the Shay Ground.

Today Chevin Edge is all but forgotten. The penny trams have long since rumbled their way into oblivion and a circle of semi-detached houses called Chevin Crescent cover the actual zoo site. Down in Salterhebble stands Elephant Terrace, a mute reminder of when Jumbo once took his daily walk.

"There's noo-an a bird alive as knows Friday neet from any other!"

A MAN'S car stalled on a country road one morning. When the man got out to fix it, a cow came along and stopped beside him. "Your trouble is probably in the carburetor," said the cow.

Startled, the man jumped back and ran down the road until he met a farmer. The amazed man told the farmer his story.

"Was it a large red cow with a brown spot over the right eye?" asked the farmer. "Yes, yes," the man replied.

"Oh! I wouldn't listen to Bessie," said the farmer. "She doesn't know a thing about cars."

A HUSBAND and wife were driving down a country lane on their way to visit some friends. They came to a muddy patch in the road and the car became bogged. After a few minutes of trying to get the car out by themselves, they saw a young farmer coming down the lane, driving some oxen before him.

The farmer stopped when he saw the couple in trouble and offered to pull the car out of the mud for £50. The husband accepted and minutes later the car was free.

The farmer turned to the husband and said: "You know, you're the tenth car I've helped out of the mud today."

The husband looked around at the fields incredulously and asked the farmer:

"When do you have time to plough your land? At night?"

"No," the young farmer replied seriously. "Night is when I put the water in the hole."

"It seems daft ter me to live poor, so that tha' can dee rich."

AN OLD lady was visiting an optician. He explained that she was sadly blind in one eye but he could help with the other eye.

She retorted: "Reet then – but think on that tha nobbut charges half price."

105

A CONCERT and dance at Buckden was once one of the great occasions of the year for junketing and merry-making.

From all parts of the dale they came: some on horse-back, some in traps, some walked – even over the tops from Littondale. The fare was varied and the audience enthusiastic; every turn was recalled.

A young lady when asked the title of her second song, whispered to Mr Anderton – who presided – *Louisiana Lou* which he misinterpreted and announced as *Lucy on the Loose*. An old Irish labourer sang *The Hat Me Father Wore*, a sort of genealogical history of his battered old hat. This raised roars of laughter and the audience joined lustily in the chorus, with which they were familiar as he had been singing the same song for the last forty years.

During the interval everyone was regaled with mulled ale containing eggs and spices.

And then the dance; such robust merrymaking is not seen nowadays. Amongst the dances were the Square Eight, Meeting Six, Cheer up Sam and the Ribbon Dance, and what energy was put into them. When some of the revellers arrived home it would be time to start the morning's work on the farm.

WAITRESS AT country inn, to diner who has instucted her to hand dishes on the left:

"Eh, luv, are ye superstitious?"

"It wouldn't break."

YOUNG JIMMY wanting to work on a farm, was advised to see farmer Grimley not far from where he lived. So an interview was arranged and Grimley finally said:

"You seem OK to me Jimmy lad, but I will have to take up your references. Come and see me in a week's time".

When Jimmy called later Grimley said:

"I have had good references about you and you can start in the morning."

To which Jimmy replied: "I've 'ad references 'bout you an' all, an' I anner cum."

Bees

I love bees.
Such pretty, busy things:
They fly a million missions
With their tiny fragile wings.
In and out of roses
Snapdragons and sweet peas.
The pollen count is very high
I wonder, do bees sneeze?

A LITTLE girl was talking to her teacher about whales. The teacher said it was physically impossible for a whale to swallow a human because even though it was a very large mammal its throat was very small. The little girl stated that Jonah was swallowed by a whale. Irritated, the teacher reiterated that a whale could not swallow a human; it was physically impossible. The little girl said:

"When I get to heaven I will ask Jonah."

The teacher asked: "What if Jonah went to hell?"

The little girl replied: "Then you ask him."

IN THE days when beggars were common even in towns, a well-known and wealthy Leeds businessman was stopped by a traditional beggar outside Leeds Town Hall. He brushed aside the beggar, saying:

"I can't give you anything now. I'll be back later."

The beggar observed:

"It's me giving credit to men like that, keeps me poor."

A SUNDAY school teacher was discussing the Ten Commandments with her five- and six-year-olds. After explaining the commandment to 'honour' thy Father and thy Mother, she asked:

"Is there a commandment that teaches us how to treat our brothers and sisters?"

Without missing a beat one little boy (the oldest of a large family) answered: "Thou shall not kill."

ONE DAY a little girl was sitting and watching her mother do the dishes at the kitchen sink. She suddenly noticed that her mother had several strands of white hair sticking out in contrast on her brunette head. She looked at her mother and inquisitively asked:

"Why are some of your hairs white, Mum?"

Her mother replied: "Well, every time that you do something wrong and make me cry or unhappy, one of my hairs turns white."

The little girl thought about this revelation for a while and then said: "Mummy, how come ALL of grandma's hairs are white?"

A COAL dealer who used to operate at Clapham station was so keen to deliver the exact weight that he kept a row of assorted cobs of coal near the scales to ensure perfect balance.

A TEACHER was giving a lesson on the circulation of the blood. Trying to make the matter clearer, she said:

"Now, class, if I stood on my head, the blood, as you know, would run into it, and I would turn red in the face."

"Yes," the class said.

"Then why is it that while I am standing upright in the ordinary position the blood doesn't run into my feet?"

A little fellow shouted: "Cos your feet aren't empty."

OVERHEARD ON a Grassington to Skipton bus.

"Ee luv, Ah feels reight 'olla inside."

"Aye," was the reply. "That's t' worst of eatin' nowt on an empty stomach."

A SWALEDALE man bought a very secondhand car and took his friends for a drive. It even struggled on down-hill stretches and crawled up hills. Then something passed them.

"Wot were that?" asked the driver.

"Nay I don't kna," replied one of the passengers. "I think it were a traction engine."

"Excuse us, but you've stopped EXACTLY on a right of way…"

NOTICE TO kitchen staff:

"Would ladies please rinse out tea pots then stand upside down in the sink. On no account must hot bottoms be put on the worktops."

IN THE West Riding a man called in at a pub and ordered a glass of beer.

"Looks like rain," said the friendly landlord.

"Aye," was the reply. "An' that's wot it tastes like."

"Hay fever?
"No, pop festival."

RICHARD BRAITHWAITE (1588-1673) was an odd character, and his book *Barnabee Itinerarium*, generally translated as *Drunken Barnaby's Journal* or *Drunken Barnaby's Four Journeys to the North of England*, is certainly a very unusual book. Probably there is nothing closely comparable in the whole of English literature.

Of all Braithwaite's enormous literary output only this one has survived. All the rest of his fifty-odd volumes are dead and well buried. No one reads them, and very few of us have ever heard of them. The Journal, however, is as alive today as it was when it first appeared in 1638.

The 'Old Ballad of Barnabee' which gives its name to this book, seems to have eluded all researches, though there are mentions of it at various dates between 1621 and 1729. The only lines of the original now known are:

> *Barnaby, Barnaby, thou'st been drinking,*
> *(I can tell by thy nose and they eyes winking)*
> *Drunk at Richmond, Drunk at Dover*
> *Drunk at Newcastle, and drunk all over.*
> Chorus
> *Whoop, Barnaby, take 't for a warning*
> *The drunk overnight are dry the next morning.*

Presumably, the 'whoop' is to be recited as a hiccough. Barnaby himself is apparantly a myth and the name was adopted by Braithwaite as that of a hero symbolising all drunkards.

Yorkshire Makes Sense of Work
Muriel F Burgess

*The SIGHT of the mills with their chimneys
so tall,*
*To HEAR all the tunes chimed by Bradford
Town Hall*
*The fine FEEL of worsted that's made in
Lumb Lane*
*The SMELL of new wool when you're
caught in the rain*
*But the final sensation which makes life so
good*
*Is the TASTE of roast beef and a real
Yorkshire Pud!*

A TOWN teacher was giving her first lesson to a class of nine-year olds in an upland farm area.

She had chosen as her subject 'Wool' and began by showing a large coloured picture of a sheep and remarking:

"Now, I am sure you all know what this is."

To this there was no response.

So she asked the question more directly.

After another pause one of the boys asked if he could see the picture more closely. Permission being given, he examined it carefully then said:

"It's a two-year-old Border Leicester, isn't it?"

TWO OLD village lads, each more than seventy, were regular customers of the pub. Their red noses denoted their hobby.

One day they saw an advertisement in the paper: "Red noses cured – send five shillings."

So they got five bob together for the remedy and back came the reply:

"Keep drinking until it turns blue."

And they did.

THE FOUR ages of man:
1. You believe in Santa Claus.
2. You don't believe in Santa Claus.
3. You are Santa Claus.
4. You look like Santa Claus.

FOR NO apparent reason the local preacher suddenly burst out laughing in the middle of his sermon. It was some time before he could control himself and then, after apologising for his unseemly behaviour, he explained:

"There's 'owd John 'Arker just gone past, wi' is best Sunday claes on, and a bucket o' pig swill on 'is head, an' t' bottoms comed 'oot."

Modern-day cooks shy of using offal but daleswomen used to say "tha uses all on t' pig 'cept the squeak".

AN OLD farmer, who had led an intemperate life, lay dying. The minister was brought and, noticing the anxious look on the farmer's face, said:

"I am indeed pleased to see that you are not afraid to meet your maker."

"Nay, Nay," replied the farmer. "It's nooar Him I'm afeared of, it's t' other bloke."

AT THE annual farmers' dinner an old Dales farmer was offered Gorgonzola cheese. After a close inspection, he put it in his mouth, chewed it and spit it out.

"Have you never tasted it before?" he was asked.

"No, nivver tasted the stuff afore," was the reply, "but I've often trod on it."

CHARLES WATERTON, the eighteenth-century Wakefield-born naturalist, was in Rome one day and was, as he put it 'bored'. He climbed to the top of St Peter's and fitted a glove onto the lightning conductor. The Pope was affronted, and a contrite Waterton repeated the climb and removed the glove.

'MULLOXED' IS a good word to use just now to describe people who are muddled and confused by a multitude of jobs. Many a farmer is mulloxed by the number of forms he has to fill in.

IT HAD been a hot dry summer, but on the moors, where the peat hags and the soft swampy hollows had been warmed up nourished by the sunshine, the herbage was more succulent and plentiful. Lambs were coming in from the hills in good condition.

This was the subject under discussion by a number of Teesdale farmers, when one said: "Fell lambs are good this back end."

"Aye," replied another. "They're allus good when they've bin roasted twice – yance on t' earth and yance in t' oven."

THE 'QUACK' doctor of the 1940s was among a cast of amazing, and preposterous, characters claiming to cure all ills and ailments who set up shop in Bradford's John Street Market – so much so that it became known as the Quack Market.

There was some speculation he had been struck off the Medical Register, or at least had some medical knowledge but not the qualification. He would set up his pitch, involving a straight-backed chair, and would offer to remove cataracts painlessly – for a price, of course, of under ten shillings.

Surprisingly, there was always a queue from the many people who gathered to watch him 'operate'. Patients would be led to the chair and seated. The 'doctor' would gargle red-coloured liquid from a bottle before licking, again and again, the clouded eyeball. He would then spit out into a bucket.

TIMID COUNTRYWOMAN in town, watching beacon flash at pedestrian crossing:

"They don't give you much time to get across, do they?"

A BRADFORD fishmonger, who had just come back from his holiday, was complimented on how well he looked and how he had got so brown:

"It's rust from t' rain."

Pancake Tuesday
M T Waller

We raced each other home at noon:
Ignorin' t' rain and mud:
It meant 'at t' year were drawin' near
To t' bluebell time, in t' wood.
If t' snow came back to-morrow
We'ed think it nearly spring:
No matter if we felt half froze
We'd hed us pankcake fling.

A PUPIL in a Dales school gave this definition of a Quaker:

"A Quaker is a man at nivver grumbles, nivver wants to feight an' nivver answers back. My feither's a Quaker but mi muther isn't."

WHILST TAKING a country walk on Boxing Day a couple came to a large gate which they found difficult to open.

"Push it hard," shouted a dalesman.

They did but as they walked through the gateway he remarked:

"Ah can see tha' didn't hev Yorkshire pudding with tha' turkey yesterday."

"I see this one is down as 'self-cooker' only!"

AN OLD lady out for a drive in her first car stopped at a Dales garage and asked for a longer dipstick. When asked why she replied: "Because it doesn't reach the oil."

AN ANGLER in Swaledale was accosted by a very irate landowner for fishing on his private water. He was told that he should be fishing in the water half a mile upstream.

"Reet," was the reply. "I'll bide here 'till t' watter gets here."

"I'll have the best fishing story of them all."

HERBERT BALER left school in 1914 and became an apprentice to the grocery trade and was concerned with high class tea and coffee within the premises at Ousegate in York. He was taught to blend tea and roast coffee beans. There was a special day to do the tea blending, using a large, hand-operated drum to rotate the tea. It was a terrible dusty job and he finished the day covered from head to foot in thick brown dust. He was unable to breathe properly for the rest of the week. He also wore a paper flour bag to protect his head.

In those days the tea was wrapped flat in special printed tea paper weighed in pounds, half-pounds and quarters. They used tall, old-fashioned scales, with a tea paper folded at the weight end as a tare. After being wrapped, it was fastened with white cotton string and Herbert tied a grocer's knot, which he could still do at the age of eighty-two. His employer had tea-tasting seasons from samples sent in by competing suppliers. He would still use the occasional brew of leaf tea, but how much simpler it is, he said, to grab a tea bag, which was only invented after the Second World War.

A CRUSTY old Whitby sailor describing his toothache:

"'Tis from t' foremost grinder aloft on t' starboard side."

FARMWORKER TO his wife, observing the work of the Electricity Generating Board: "Look, dear, them electric pythons are coming across our valley."

SARAH AND JOE lived in a back-to-back house in one of the cobbled streets before t' pictures and t' wireless. All the kids were in bed, and Joe had just got nice and comfortable in front of a blazing fire, when Sarah joined him and said: "Joe, dusta think we could 'ave a pianner?"

Next day, being a Saturday, Joe took the tram to town, went into a piano shop and said he wanted to buy one.

"What kind do you require?" asked the salesman.

"Nay lad," replied Joe. "Ah don't know aht abah't 'em; thee pick yan fer me cos none of us can play yan."

"Well then," said the young man. "What you want is a pianola – if you will step this way I'll show you one. You don't have to learn to play – anyone can use it."

Joe could not get home quickly enough to tell Sarah what was coming.

"I've gitten someat better, it's a pianola."

"What's that?" she asked.

"Well lass, it's just reet for us. Ah can use it, tha' can use it, Billy, Millie, Albert and Fred can use it – we can all use it."

Sarah glared at him and shouted:

"An' I expect it'll be me wot has to empty it."

An old dalesman's advice about hiring a gardener: "Tha' mun goh by 'is trousis. If they're patched on t' nees you want 'im. If they're patched on't seat yer don't."

"You'd fly fast, too, with your tail on fire."

Me Muther's weshed t' doorst'nes
An t' flegs's bin done:
An' t' steps fair shinin'
Shoo's scaared ivv'ry one.
She cum in an' warned me
As Ah stood o' t' rug.
"Thee mucky them steps
An Ah'll rattle thee lug,"
Ah want to goa laikin'
Ha' can Ah get aht
Ah'd fly ower t' lot
If Ah'd wings – but I'm baht.
Ah c'uld jump ower t' steps
Aye. Ah thinks as Ah will;
An' afore shees fun aht
Ah'll be hawf way dahn t' hill.

WHEN MEN wrote romantically about the Dales they peopled the hidden village of Thorpe near Grassington with cobblers. The number of craftsmen were given as 42, 52 or even 60. J H Dixon, writing in 1853, says that "Thorpe is famous for the quality of its shoes and boots". By this time shoe-making was becoming more and more industrialised and the famous Cobblers of Thorpe were passing into history.

THESE DAYS many Dalesfolk are well read but this was not always the case. When an old-time dalesman was told that he was going to be given a book for his birthday he replied:

"Don't thee bother thissen – I've got one."

In those far-off days a Dales farmer would have a library consisting of a Bible, a guide to local sheep marks and a farm stock book. He would, of course, have his bank book in pride of place.

FARMER, GAZING at a very gnarled oak tree, reflecting on the local belief that trees grow crooked in the light of the moon:

"Reckon he grew in t' dark as well as in moonlight."

MIDDLE-AGED woman at the grocer's:

"Me 'usband, 'is 'air's grey mostly, but 'e washed it in Zomo an' 'e come out white as a badger."

"Somebody has cut the appendix out of this book."

OBSERVED AN old farmworker:

"I only once took a holiday, as you might say – when mi wife went off wi' t' lodger."

The Farmer's Prayer

Let the lordly and great roll by in their state
I envy them not I declare it
I have my own lamb, my own chicken and ham
I shear my own fleece and I wear it
I have fruit, I have flowers
I have lawns, I have bowers
The lark is my morning alarmer
So, jolly boys now, here's to God speed the plough
Long life and success to the farmer

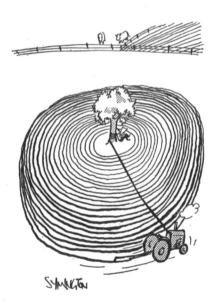

SYMINGTON